Praise for *Ign.*

"Chris gets real and shares an inspiring story of how he went from disabled from ten back surgeries to finding his true purpose in life and creating a movement that is helping people unlock the secret to living a fulfilled life."

—Dave Jesiolowski, author of *One Decision Can*, former professional hockey player who finished top 100 all-time in penalty minutes

"I have seen firsthand what Chris has done and I am amazed by his resilience and passion for helping people become who God created them to be."

—Ted DiBiase Jr., professional wrestler and movie star

"Chris Kellum guides you on a journey to discover, understand and claim your God-given purpose; igniting the greatness within each of us and leads to a truly fulfilling life that transcends the demands and distractions of the everyday."

—Adam Such, retired Green Beret and servant

IGNITING YOUR PURPOSE

DISCOVER AND BECOME WHO GOD CREATED YOU TO BE

CHRIS KELLUM

Kellum Brothers

ISBN: 9781730801532

Printed in the United States of America.

Ordering information
To order a copy of this book go to kellumbrothers.com or call (769) 300-1294
Bulk order discounts available

To Jesus, who I owe everything, and to those whose lives have been rocked by a disability.

TABLE OF CONTENTS

PROLOGUE

Confused by the abrupt ending of a long and successful medical sales career, I was now terrified at having been placed on long-term disability and the uncertainty of what was next. Now, in the midst of an identity crisis, I was lost and desperately searching for answers.

Eighteen months earlier, Polly and I had joined up with an amazing group of people and helped start Bellwether Church where I was serving as worship leader. Bellwether Church became my refuge and was a time for which I am forever grateful as the church body loved on us and walked us through incredibly difficult circumstances.

Life-long friendships were made and these friendships helped guide my family into the next season of our lives. A season that became unbelievably more difficult than anything I had ever been through.

During this time Chris Snopek, Todd Dyess, Kevin Kellum (my twin brother), Keith Lofton, and I grabbed our families and spent the weekend at Ole Miss watching baseball. One Saturday morning during breakfast in a coffee shop led to a vision of a 3–4 day sports camp for teenage boys that would combine sports training, music, and summer camp activities. This sounded like a great idea considering Chris and Todd were both professional baseball players!

After getting home, I shared the idea with my friend Dobby Bowdon and all I heard was, "I'm in, brother. ALL IN!"

We soon built an incredible team and began meeting weekly for prayer and planning sessions. The following August, we launched our first IGNITE sports camp with 50% of the campers coming from local schools and 50% coming from inner-city schools through organizations we partnered with and gave scholarships for admission.

Camp was full of young men from different races, cultures, and socio-economic backgrounds. Teenagers initially focused on the different worlds from which they came, yet within a few short hours all that changed as they shared life together. Barriers were shattered and walls broken down as their common love for sports brought them closer together and gave life to lasting friendships still seen today.

What I witnessed, and was privileged to be a part of, was unlike anything I'd ever experienced before. Four days later as I began driving off the campground, completely exhausted, I knew I would never be the same. Somehow, the man who arrived at the IGNITE sports camp was not the man leaving. I had changed.

As I approached the end of that dusty gravel road, I stopped on top of the hill to look back and think about the weekend. Suddenly, tears came streaming down my face as I came to grips with what I had just experienced. It was a heaviness I could not contain nor control. I knew right then that something significant had just been born.

Helping start IGNITE and Bellwether were defining moments

in my life. Years of serving others through them is how I discovered my purpose of helping people discover and become who God created them to be.

I want to ask you to allow me to take you on this journey to discovering and becoming who God created you to be. We may not know each other personally, but I believe, with everything in me, there's greatness inside of you and it's found in your true purpose. The purpose God put within you is bigger than anything you can imagine. Your purpose is your greatness and I respectfully want to help lead you to it.

I'm just a guy who's been blessed to find his purpose through some unusual circumstances. Just a man blessed by the Lord to live a lot of different lives that ultimately led me to the life He created me for.

Where are you today? What are you searching for? Do you feel like you're winning in this game of life? Will you take this journey with me? I certainly hope so.

Now let's turn the page and start discovering and becoming who God created you to be!

PART 1: Awareness

Chapter 1
FROM PAIN TO PURPOSE

"Pain is meant to wake us up. People try to hide their pain. But they're wrong. Pain is something to carry, like a radio. You feel your strength in the experience of pain."

—JIM MORRISON

THE PAIN

Something wasn't right, and I knew it even though I didn't want to admit it.

The pain had gotten significantly worse and had become harder and harder to fight through each day. I saw the look in Dr. McGuire's eyes as he walked into the room. This time, however, Dr. McGuire, one of the coolest dudes I know, wasn't carrying that big smile he usually walked in with. This time was different and I could tell he was choosing his words carefully.

Eighteen months earlier, he performed my eighth back surgery, a three-level lumbar fusion. I had been in that exam room many times for checkups and scans, and I always loved how Dr. McGuire followed the same routine each time he walked in. Right when I was thinking, *Why didn't he walk to the computer screen?* I heard, "Hey Chris, is Polly here today?" That's when I knew something was seriously wrong.

Those carefully chosen words, which we'll discuss later in the book, ended with him putting me on long-term disability at 38 years old and as much as I wanted to disagree, deep down I knew he was right, and I trusted him completely. The truth is I was tired, and at that point, the pain was winning—at least that's how I saw it and I HATE losing!

THE DEFINING MOMENT

Little did I know, the message he crafted so intently for me that day would be the same words that would later help provide the strength I'd need to fight the battle that so patiently waited for me. A battle that I highly underestimated.

Walking out of the exam room that day was tough, and I still remember every detail of the visit. The faint smell of an antiseptic and the clicking sound of a worn-out computer keyboard are forever cemented in my brain. The worst was the fear of leaving the clinic. I'd somehow convinced myself that when I walked outside the building, it would be the official end of the career I so dearly loved. *Is this real? Am I dreaming?* I thought. Cautiously, I stepped out.

At that moment everything around me seemed to change as my normal quickly slipped away. The ten-minute car ride home felt like hours. What would I do? How would I break this to my family? My wife? Would they be ashamed of me? Would they be embarrassed by me? How would they respect a father, a husband who can't provide for them? How would I respect myself?

These questions and thoughts overwhelmed me and nothing

I did could stop them as **they violently attacked me at my very core.** The feelings and the fears were new to me and something I'd never experienced. My mind kicked into overdrive as I desperately searched for a way to fix it, but there was nothing I could do. Nothing.

John Maxwell says that significance is usually found after periods of being stretched in life. He uses the analogy of a rubber band. Unless a rubber band is stretched, it can't be used for its true purpose. Well, I was being stretched! We were being stretched! Bad! I felt like Stretch Armstrong, a toy popular in the '70s that had the ability to stretch up to fifteen inches. Everything in and around me was being stretched. My world, at times, felt like it was falling apart. Honestly, at times it was. The truth is John's right. That stretching, as painful as it was, did exactly what he said it would.

In the end, it led me to **discover and become who God created me to be.** It walked me right into my Why.

I know that sounds nuts but it's true, and waking up each day knowing that is something I'm incredibly thankful for. I'm thankful for the ten back surgeries, endless spinal epidurals, days and days of pain, mountains of medical bills, losing my job, and being put on disability. On and on it goes and yet I wouldn't take back a single day, because it's worth it.

Why? **Because discovering and becoming who God created you to be is the key to living a fulfilled life.** Waking up with clarity and knowing your true purpose makes every day a blessing to wake up to. I tell this to people all the time and they trip out and usually look at me like I'm certified crazy, but what's crazy about it? What's crazy about living the life God created you for? I'd argue that living any other way is insane.

I hear people over and over again searching for their purpose in life and it's simple. **Our purpose is to take the strengths, gifts, passions, and desires God has put within us and use them to bring glory to Him.** As simple as that may sound, it's often not so easy to identify within ourselves on how to accomplish that.

For years I'd been excited about who I was, my accomplishments, the job I had, and the life I was living. Then because of my back surgeries, I was forced to ACCEPT drastic changes to my circumstances and the identity I had held on to for so long. **Change is scary because you are forced to confront the unknown.**

I believe God's Word and it says in Romans 8:28: *And we know that in ALL THINGS God works for the good of those who love Him, who have been called according to His purpose.* I know that all the pain and problems I've had with my back and becoming disabled (even though I refuse to use that word!), enabled me to find my true passion and purpose in life.

MY PURPOSE

If you ask me today what that purpose is, I immediately say, **"To help people discover and become who God created them to be."** I can also quickly shout out the values I live by daily as well as my six daily declarations. It took having to go through living hell to do so. It took, as Jim Morrison so eloquently said, pain to get me there. **The pain was the catalyst that led me down the road to a purpose-led life.** I was now living my life on purpose.

The pain, uncomfortableness, and disability slowed me down long enough to see that I was given an OPPORTUNITY to view life from a different perspective. A perspective of pain, that I now use to connect with others to help them take their pain, in whatever form it takes, and use it to move them to discover and become who God created them to be.

Pain is one of the greatest catalysts for transformation in our lives.

Now that I was grounded from disability, I spent most of my time each day at Bellwether. I read tons of material and worked hard on becoming a better musician, speaker, and communicator. I became keenly aware of a change happening in me that caused me to begin paying close attention to the things I felt a deep connection with and I wasn't even sure why. Writing down these connections was just something I knew I was supposed to do. So I did.

For some reason, I kept most of this to myself and told no one what was going on inside me. What was I afraid of? This time consisted of many highs and lows and I was learning things about myself I never knew. This was surprising because I assumed I knew everything there was to know about me and discovering new passions and strengths, as well as weaknesses and fears, was not something I was expecting at 38 years old.

I could feel the transformation going on inside me and there were days I was excited about it and days I was truly scared to death and some days my head felt like it was spinning in circles. Many times, even though I trusted what the Lord was doing, I struggled to process what was going on. I would often wake up to a wall of pain and fear and the faint sniffles of my wife Polly failing to hold back her tears as we faced the mounds of medical bills and stress of the situation. This made things cloudy and had us just trying to make it through the day.

Some days were great and other days I felt like an epic failure as I watched Polly work herself to death so we could make ends meet. I struggled with this transformation.

What about you? Where are you in life right now? Are you in the middle of a painful transformation? Can you identify with our situation? Maybe you're in a place where you feel like you're living day to day with no passion or just living for the weekends. Trust me, pay close attention to the changes happening in and around you. Also, recognize and accept this time of transformation.

Years ago, Polly and I were in Europe and went to a glass factory where we watched a man use fire to make a beautiful vase which, at first glance, looked perfect. The long-legged glass blower, with his thick silver beard, deep voice, and an obvious passion for his work, saw tiny imperfections in the vase that we could not see.

Grabbing the vase, he placed it back in the fire and, after turning fiery red, he began to work with it in ways that, at the time, didn't make sense to us. After several minutes of twisting, blowing, and twirling the fiery ball of red, he pulled out the vase and it was ABSOLUTELY BEAUTIFUL. Everyone around was amazed by its beauty.

Just like the man sculpting the vase, not everything starts out perfect. You most likely will have to go back and work on those imperfections until one day everyone around you is amazed at the beauty you have created.

The very thing you are most afraid of right now might be what you're thanking God for in the near future.

Why?

Because **transformation, however it comes, is what walks you into becoming the person you are meant to be.**

It did for me.

What about you?

How will you use times of transformation to help you grow?

"Just when the caterpillar thought the world was over, it became a butterfly."

—PROVERB

FOCUS AND IMPLEMENTATION REMINDERS:

Pain is one of the greatest catalysts for transformation in our lives.

Transformation, however it comes, is what walks you into becoming the person you are meant to be.

Much like a rubber band, it takes being stretched to find your true purpose.

Our purpose is to take the strengths, gifts, passions, and desires that God has put within us and use them to bring glory to Him.

Your purpose is the key to living a fulfilled life.

NEW APPROACH:

Embrace change, walk boldly into the unknown, and approach your purpose with confidence!

Chapter 2
THE POWER OF WORDS

"Have you realized that most of your unhappiness in life is due to the fact that you are listening to yourself instead of talking to yourself?"

—DAVID MARTYN LLOYD-JONES

With confidence falling off every word, he looked me straight in the eyes and said, "Chris, you're wired like those Navy SEALs I've worked with and you can do this."

Those are the carefully chosen words from Dr. McGuire the day he put me on long-term disability and he said them to me right before we walked out of his office. Those words didn't seem like much at the time and the way he spoke them was as if he was giving them life for me to grab hold of one day. He did give them life and I grabbed hold of them countless times and still do to this day.

I can't count the number of times I thought about giving up because that's what pain does to you. It's brutal and can be mental torture. When it would happen though, I would remember what Dr. McGuire said to me and what God says about me and use that strength to push through it.

Now I don't pretend to know what it takes to have the mental strength of a Navy SEAL. Not even close! The level of respect I have for the special forces of the United States military is off the chart. Those guys are my heroes and that's exactly what made those words so special and powerful to me. To be compared to my heroes gave me a new mindset—it gave me hope!

Since that day, I've paid careful attention to the words I use when speaking to others and myself. Each word we use has life to either lift up or tear down. I want to lift people up and I want to be lifted up. The voice in your head can and will determine the trajectory of your thoughts, which influences your actions, which determines your results in all areas of your life. Choose your words carefully and they will determine your future.

What words live in you?

Let's do this exercise. With each topic below, take one minute and write down words you associate with each. Do this using a timer on your phone or watch and write as fast as you can for the full minute per topic. Ready?

1. Yourself
2. Your life
3. Your job
4. Your boss

Now pay close attention to the words you wrote to describe your life. What do they look like? How do they make you feel? Are they positive or negative? Do they lift up or tear down?

Since 2008, we've brought in professional athletes as speakers at IGNITE camps and I've yet to meet one that doesn't focus on the words they speak to themselves. Why? Because they know the power of words and how negative words bring negative actions. The words you speak dictate how you see life and yourself which can dictate your destiny.

This is nothing new. In fact, we see it in the Bible. Moses sent spies to check out the Promised Land and all but two, Joshua and Caleb, came back with words of negativity. Because of that, Joshua and Caleb were the only two out of thousands of people to enter the Promised Land.

Negative words bring negative results. PERIOD.

Dr. Maxwell Maltz, in his book *Psycho-Cybernetics* said, *"You act, and feel, not according to what things are really like, but according to the image your mind holds of what they are like. You have certain mental images of yourself, your world, and the people around you, and you behave as though these images were the truth, the reality, rather than the things they represent."*

The words we speak to ourselves and others help shape self-image.

Dr. Maltz also said, *"The self-image is the key to human personality and human behavior. Change the self-image and you change the personality and the behavior ... The self-image sets the boundaries of individual accomplishment. It defines what you can and cannot do. Expand the self-image and you expand the area of the possible."*

If our self-image is shaped by the words we use, and it drives our success then why would we ever speak in ways that could put limitations on ourselves? **There is POWER in positive words and we have got to STOP self-imposing limitations on our own lives.**

You were created to soar and greatness lies in the details. Begin changing your life today by speaking positive words and watch them begin to change your life and maybe even the lives of others. I'm certainly thankful that Dr. McGuire chose this route because his choice of words helped change my life.

Think about it. A life changed by one sentence.

What will your next sentence be?

"Promise yourself that you will talk health, happiness, and prosperity as often as possible."

—JOHN WOODEN

FOCUS AND IMPLEMENTATION REMINDERS:

Words have lives of truth or deceit.

The words you speak dictate how you see life and YOURSELF.

Negative words = negative results.

The words we speak to ourselves AND others help shape self-image.

Self-image is the key to human personality AND human behavior.

Self-image sets the boundaries of individual accomplishment and defines what you can and cannot do.

NEW APPROACH:

Begin and end each day by speaking five "I am" statements to yourself while looking in the mirror. "I am" statements are positive and encouraging truths about YOU that focus on your strengths!

Chapter 3
FINDING A NEW WHY

"Life is a matter of choices, and every choice you make makes you."

—JOHN C. MAXWELL

Perry's eyes were as bright as the stars outside as he stood before his peers at an IGNITE sports camp declaring his new-found love for the Lord. It was exciting to see a 15-year-old young man who faced so many struggles, feeling free and unchained from the burdens he was carrying when he arrived. Soon after that, I found myself outside trying to decide where the screaming was coming from, and as I made my way to the source I realized it was Perry. I was caught off guard at the chaos and Perry, with his sunken head in his hands, screaming as my friends Todd and Dobby tried to console him.

"I can't do this no more! I can't do this no more!" Perry screamed as he beat his head with his hands.

"What Perry? What's wrong?" Todd and Dobby fired back.

"I can't do this no more! I can't do it!" Perry sobbed as his body started to collapse.

"Why Perry? What's wrong? Tell me why?" I begged.

"I can't do this no more...Because I know...Because I know," he cried.

"Perry, please tell us what's going on?" Dobby asked.

The silence seemed to last forever. Finally, we heard, "My momma makes me steal from people, so she can feed my baby sister and I can't do that no more... Because I know." As Perry looked at the three of us with tears pouring from his eyes he dropped his head in his hands and softly said: "Because I know."

Todd, Dobby, and I held on to Perry as our hearts lay broken. Perry had come to a crossroad unlike anything I'd ever seen. Nothing from our sheltered upbringings had prepared us for that and nothing in us could relate to what Perry was going through. All we could do was listen and be there for him, so that's what we did. In the end, that's exactly what Perry needed.

That exact moment in time is one I'll never forget as we witnessed a young man **coming to terms with his new *Why.*** A why of loving and serving the Lord and a why that was now inconsistent with his old self. A why that demanded a new **APPROACH** and that's exactly what Perry did.

I've thought back to that night quite often over the years and I'm still amazed by the courage Perry showed. **It takes courage to live the life and purpose you know God has called you to live.** As with Perry, often sacrifices must be made and they're not always easy and sometimes very painful.

Are you facing a "Because I know" circumstance? Are you in the middle of some potentially big sacrifices? Are you, like Perry, at a crossroad?

If so, what are you going to do about it? How are you going to handle it? Will you face it head on like Perry and find a new approach or will you avoid it and possibly allow it to keep you from the life you've been called to? The life you were specifically created for?

Perry taught me a valuable lesson. If I woke up tomorrow with no back pain, no rods in my back, and had the opportunity to go back to my old job I wouldn't do it. I couldn't do it.

Why?

I now know who God created me to be.

Getting here was a long road but it's a road I'd gladly travel again and again. You see my pain brought my purpose and as I continue to grow into the man He created me to be, there's nothing else I could ever imagine doing.

Why?

Because I know. Do you?

"Take delight in the Lord because He will give you the desires of your heart."

—PSALM 37:4

FOCUS AND IMPLEMENTATION REMINDERS:

It takes courage to live the life you were created to live.

Living your Why often requires a new approach.

Each step you take in faith towards your Why will empower you to take another.

Faith Steps produce the awareness needed to discover your Why.

NEW APPROACH:

With each day do two things.

1. Take or plan a Faith Step.

2. Keep a detailed awareness journal of the connections you felt with each step towards your purpose.

Chapter 4
PURSUING FULFILLMENT

"Success without fulfillment is the ultimate failure."

—TONY ROBBINS

Growing up in Atlanta, Georgia, Jason Cook dreamed of playing in the NFL. After receiving a scholarship to play football at Ole Miss, he was one step closer to accomplishing that dream. In the fall of 2009, after a standout college career, Jason was drafted by the Baltimore Ravens. His dream had become a reality.

Jason was the headline speaker at several of our IGNITE sports camps and I'll never forget the story of his first NFL touchdown that happened to be against the Atlanta Falcons, his hometown team.

"We had to drive the full length of the field towards the end zone where all my friends and family were sitting," he said with a big smile.

"We hit the left, then the right and we were doing it, man! With every snap, we got closer and closer to the goal, to my people. I remember everything about it and I could hear my family screaming my name!

"As we approached the goal I got the call … Cook to the left. I took the handoff and with every step, the goal got closer and closer and crossing that goal line was crazy! I mean CRAZY!! Every emotion went racing through my mind as I thought about all the hours, days, and years I'd trained for that one thing. Since I was a little boy I'd dreamed of that moment! I couldn't believe it and could hear my friends and family going nuts!" Cook described.

"That's when it hit me. *That's it?* I thought. *That's what I trained my entire life for? That's what I gave blood, sweat, and tears for? That's it?* And it was right then that I knew my NFL career was over. I knew," Jason paused, "that I had to walk away. And I did."

The room, packed full of future NFL hopefuls, sat in silence, completely stunned at what they had just heard.

Why would Jason step away? Why would he give up what he had worked for his entire life? What would pull him away? To most people, money, fame, TV, autographs, etc. is all you could ever want!

What causes people to do things like that? From time to time we hear similar stories to this and so often can't wrap our heads around *why* they'd do it. What would you have done? Do you know?

Do you know the difference between happiness and fulfillment? Have you ever thought about it?

Happiness is an emotional state caused by a temporary boost of serotonin and dopamine. The other day after my stretching routine I was SUPER happy until I pulled a muscle in my neck as I got up and that happiness quickly vanished.

Fulfillment, on the other hand, is a consistent state that allows for a full range of emotions. For example, my daughter came home from college recently and I walked into the house to find my whole family together laughing and having a blast. Seeing this, I was deeply fulfilled. They could have busted into a food fight and though my emotional state would have drastically changed it would not have changed my feeling of fulfillment.

Fulfillment is what is produced by living a PURPOSE-LED life. In fact, fulfillment is what your life will always pursue with or without your recognition or acknowledgment.

Pursuing happiness, in whatever form it takes, will eventually leave you empty because happiness is a temporary state and those feelings disappear. Pursuing significance or fulfillment is a constant emotion and because of that it will leave you significantly fulfilled!

Moving from pursuing happiness to fulfillment is the first step in leading you to discover and become who God created you to be. It's powerful to see someone begin pursuing fulfillment over happiness because it changes their life and provides an explosive energy that's contagious to all around.

This step has a long history of transforming lives, businesses, cultures, and communities.

That hot Mississippi summer day when I first met Jason Cook, I had no idea his step would have such a profound impact on my life and the lives of dozens of IGNITE counselors and campers. Transformation seemed to follow him as his Why was contagious to anyone around.

Jason is no doubt living his Why and it's felt by everyone around him. There's one thing I know for sure. He'd sacrifice a million touchdowns for one day of living the life God created him for!

Why?

Because God called him to something bigger than football, fame, and fortune. He called Jason to be who He created him to be. Today Jason is a pastor for Fellowship Church in Memphis and living out his true purpose while living a fulfilled life.

What do you think God is calling you to do?

"Dear brothers, let us not love with words or speech but with actions and in truth."

—1 John 3:18

FOCUS AND IMPLEMENTATION REMINDERS:

Happiness is a TEMPORARY emotional state caused by a boost of serotonin and dopamine.

Fulfillment is a CONSISTENT state that allows for a full range of emotions.

Fulfillment is what your life will always pursue with or without your recognition or acknowledgment.

Fulfillment changes lives, provides energy, and is contagious to those around.

Fulfillment is what is produced by living a purpose-led life.

NEW APPROACH:

Get alone in a quiet place each day for three to five minutes and answer these questions:

1. I find fulfillment in _____.

2. Why, specifically, does this bring me fulfillment?

Chapter 5
DISCOVER WHO GOD CREATED YOU TO BE

"Serving others breaks you free from the shackles of self and self-absorption that choke out the joy of living."

—JAMES HUNTER

Two of my good friends, WWE star Ted DiBiase Jr. and retired Green Beret Adam Such, met while filming a reality show in Alaska. Ted's been a part of the IGNITE team for years and shared it with Adam during their trip. Several months later Adam shows up in Mississippi to serve with us at the Team 8 camp and I was blown away by his willingness to do so. When I asked Adam why he came he simply said, "I was asked."

"Uh ... say what?" I replied.

"Ted asked, so I came," he said.

"So, if asked you just roll?" was all I could think to say.

Adam looked me straight in the eyes and said, "Chris whether you realize it or not, you guys are fighting for these kids and you're in a battle to show them a different way of life. I'm a warrior. It's who I am. I came to help fight. I don't have to grab a gun and go to the Middle East for a fight. I just need some brothers to fight with."

The next year Adam packed up his family and moved to Mississippi and is in the fight. Why? Because he knows his purpose. He's a warrior and fights for others. Period.

The path to fulfillment starts by serving others. When you serve others with the strengths and gifts God has given you it begins to **shine a light on small corners of your Why** as you start to discover deep connections and desires that you MUST pay attention to. As you serve and become aware of these connections write them down and ask yourself this question:

"Why, specifically, did I connect with that?"

I know this may feel weird for some of you but trust me. TAKE NOTES and document everything. By doing this you will become even more sensitive to the connections. That sensitivity leads to deep **awareness, which leads to discovery!**

Think of it like you're trying to solve a mystery and the more detailed notes you take the easier it will be to identify the crook.

As you start to identify your strengths, passions, desires, and gifts, begin to find ways to use these to serve others. Find areas in your community, schools, churches, etc. to serve. When you do you will discover new strengths, passions, and desires about yourself or your company that you didn't know you had. To do this requires one thing. **STEPPING OUT OF YOUR COMFORT ZONE.**

Are you willing to step outside your comfort zone and try something different? Something new?

We were created to serve others. When you put others

above yourself you begin to experience significance. Acts of significance lead to discovering your Why and that is where you find fulfillment.

Billy Alsbrooks says it like this, "God's calling for you is DIRECTLY tied to you using the gifts He has given you. Inside the calling is the anointing and it's the anointing that makes you unstoppable!"

"A journey of a thousand miles starts with a single step."

—LAO TZU

What's keeping you from that first step? It kills me to see men and women miserable in their jobs and living for the weekends. I can see the pain in their eyes and my fear for you is that you get to the end of your life and say, "I wish I would have...."

Poet John Greenleaf Whittier wrote, "For all sad words of tongue and pen, the saddest are these, 'It might have been.'"

Don't let the fear of discomfort keep you from your WHY! It's easy to procrastinate and keep with the daily routine of wake up, go to work, go home while focusing on making more money to buy more things. That's easy. No, that's average and **you weren't created to be average!**

Begin to answer these two questions. Spend a LOT of time on them as they become your foundation.

What are your top five core values? Why?

As I mentioned in Chapter 1, very few people can quickly and precisely articulate their values. This is a MUST as your values are the guardrails of your life.

Write down your top five core values:

1. _____
2. _____
3. _____
4. _____
5. _____

What motivates you? Why?

Recognizing your motivations may take quite some time to answer, but it will begin to clear up the muddy waters of your life. Focus heavily on *why*. When you write down the answer ask yourself why again and write down that answer. Do this a total of five times. This will get to the core of what's driving you. You'll probably be surprised by the answer. I was.

Now focus on these....

What are your top three strengths?

1. _____
2. _____
3. _____

What are the top three things you're passionate about?

1. _____
2. _____
3. _____

Why? (x5)

1. *Why?* _____

_____

2. *Why?* _____

_____

3. *Why?* _____

_____

4. *Why?* _____

_____

5. *Why?* _____

_____

What do you love so much that when you do it you lose track of time?

_____

_____

_____

Why do you love it?

_____

_____

_____

What about that connects with you?

_____

_____

_____

Why does it connect?

_____

_____

_____

Write down your top three dreams.

1. _____

2. _____

3. _____

Why are these dreams a must for you?

_____

_____

_____

If you had unlimited amounts of time and money what would you do?

_____

_____

_____

Why would you do it?

_____

_____

_____

Write down three life experiences God's given you that you could use to help others.

1. _____
2. _____
3. _____

How are you using those life experiences currently?

_____

_____

_____

If you have not used those experiences, then why not?

_____

_____

_____

Write down the top three emotions you feel when you serve others.

1. _____
2. _____
3. _____

What do you think brings about those feelings?

_____

_____

_____

What specific gifts were you using when you experienced each emotion?

_____

_____

_____

Which gift did you connect with the most? Why?

_____

_____

_____

Name three people that had a positive influence on your life.

1. _____
2. _____
3. _____

How did they influence you?

_____

_____

_____

Why was that important to you?

_____

_____

_____

What about their lives were you drawn to? Why?

_____

_____

_____

This is just a start and you'll have other questions you want to write down and answer in your journal. When you do always ask yourself "Why?" and write the answer in detail. The goal is to go deep to truly discover what's driving or motivating you. You can find more on this at kellumbrothers.com.

Discovering your purpose should not be difficult, yet I talk to people all the time that seem to be searching for some secret formula like their life is a scene from the movie *Raiders of the Lost Ark*. **Your purpose is within you and all you need to do is connect with it.** Keeping a journal of your connections expedites clarity.

Remember, you were created to serve others and the journey to your purpose starts there. That's where you'll make the connections needed for clarity.

Ken Coleman says, "In an attempt to discover their life's calling, many people wait around to see a flash of light or awake to the voice of God at two or three in the morning. **Our calling isn't something we have to search for relentlessly; it's sewn into who we are.** As we recognize our strengths we'll uncover our passions. **Where our strengths intersect with our passions, therein lies our calling.**"

That's it. Thank you, Ken!

As you begin to move into discovering and becoming who God created you to be you WILL be hit by distractions, so be prepared. You were born to be great.

"You don't have to be great to get started, but you do have to get started to be great."

—LES BROWN

FOCUS AND IMPLEMENTATION REMINDERS:

The path to fulfillment starts by serving others.

Serving others with the gifts and strengths within you begin to shine a light on small corners of your Why by making you aware of the deep connections happening in you.

Your purpose is within you and all you need to do is connect with it.

We were created to serve others.

When you put others above yourself you begin to experience significance.

Acts of significance lead to discovering your Why and that is where you find fulfillment.

NEW APPROACH:

Identify two ways to serve others daily and at the end of each week journal about your experiences.

Write them down here:

_____

_____

_____

PART 2: Approach

Chapter 6
FINDING STRENGTH

"The ultimate measure of a man is not where he stands in moments of comfort and convenience, but where he stands at times of challenge and controversy."

—MARTIN LUTHER KING JR.

Post-op was nothing new to me considering I'd been there so many times before. I felt like a pro, but this time was different, and the fight was significantly harder.

You've heard me say I see it as a game that I'm NOT willing to lose. Well, this time, as much as I hate to admit it, I was losing. Bad!

My identity was slipping away and thoughts I had never allowed in my head were now taking up residence. My fear of addiction skyrocketed as I took pain pills like candy with each pill making me feel weaker and weaker within. The spiral downward was fast and furious yet no one around me, other than Polly, had a clue.

"Who are you kidding Chris? You can't do this. The pain is only getting worse. You really think you can beat this? Be honest with yourself and accept YOU CAN'T WIN!" These thoughts came at lightning speed making me weaker and weaker with each attack.

Crying out to the Lord, my prayers seemed to fall on deaf ears. Isolated and lonely I begged Him for answers. "WHERE ARE YOU!!" I screamed within.

One evening during this time, Polly raced to the bedroom at the sounds of my screams to find me crawling on the floor in an attempt to make it to the bathroom. Broken, defeated, and crushed, I laid there at my lowest point imaginable in agonizing pain with no end in sight and scared to death. *If only they could see me now*, I thought as I remembered all the people in pain I had helped over the years. I felt like a complete fraud. A total fake.

Looking up I saw Polly as she made her way to the floor. With her hand on my face and tears in her eyes, she confidently looked at me and said, "Remember Chris, God's given you the strength and you CAN do this. You can do this. Okay?" Those words rested on me as if they came from an angel. At that moment, they did. God sent the right person at the right time to remind me that what He says in His Word is true. He is our strength.

The next day as I lay on the couch in my stillness I decided to **make a decision and have the guts to get it done! I decided right there to be who God created me to be and use His strength to fight this battle.** I decided I WOULD win this fight and nothing would stop me. **Whenever those negative thoughts came to me, I'd fight back with what God says about me.** NOTHING would stop me. I WOULD ENDURE AND PREVAIL.

In my excitement and since I was alone, I shared this life-changing moment with my awesome dog Louie as he rested just below me. He's a killer listener but didn't share in my excitement quite as I'd hoped!

I'm not sure where you are in life right now but if you're reading this book, then there's a pretty good chance you're looking for a change or are in the middle of one. You now know there is a specific purpose for your life and it's up to you to discover it. How bad do you want it?

I know that sounds like a crazy question but almost everyone says they want to, yet most give up or never try at all. **Discovering your true purpose requires overcoming obstacles and CAN be time-consuming.**

Finding it, however, is life changing.

Think about it for a while. Do you REALLY want to find your Why? Your purpose?

Now I want to ask you the same question we ask kids at IGNITE. Ready?

Are you willing to make the decision and have the guts to get it done?

YES, YOU ARE!!

There is someone out there right now waiting for YOU to discover your purpose, so you can lead THEM to theirs!!

As Polly said to me, let me say to you: Remember God's given you the strength and you CAN do this!

Your greatness lies inside you and ONLY YOU can go get it!

ARE YOU WILLING?

"Hardship often prepares ordinary people for an extraordinary destiny."

—C.S. LEWIS

FOCUS AND IMPLEMENTATION REMINDERS:

To live the life God created for you, you must first be WILLING then CHOOSE to live it by allowing NOTHING to get in your way!

You must approach your Why with fierce determination!

There is a strength in you greater than anything you can imagine.

Your GREATNESS lies inside you and ONLY YOU can go get it!

NEW APPROACH:

Live by this statement: MAKE A CHOICE AND HAVE THE GUTS TO GET IT DONE!!

Chapter 7
LIVING OUT YOUR PURPOSE

"Once you find your true purpose in life, it creates freedom for you to live your life the way it is designed to be lived."

—DAVE JESIOLOWSKI

As I type this chapter, Ishmael Harley is on a college campus not too far from here tackling the first semester of his freshman year. If you know Ish, then you can attest he's probably got a big smile on his face and trying to find a way to help someone around him. It's who he is.

Years ago, Luke Epperson, a young pastor with Hillcrest Baptist Church, took a team of people each Saturday to the apartment complex where Ish lived to hand out lunch bags with Bible verses in them. For weeks Ish thought they were crazy and would most likely end up in trouble with one of the local drug dealers.

At that time Ish was struggling and considering getting involved in things that ... well let's just say ... would be frowned upon by local law enforcement. Week after week Luke's team showed up and finally, Ish accepted one of those lunches. Little did he know that day would change his life and several lives of those around him.

Soon after that Luke put together a team and started City Church and they soon became involved with IGNITE and received several scholarships to the August sports camp. August arrived, and they headed our way. When they pulled up and piled out of the car, I met young 13-year-old Ishmael Harley and Mario Asagunia and had no idea I was looking at future IGNITE Torch Award College Scholarship winners. By the way, it's the highest honor awarded at IGNITE!

From that day forward, Ish and Mario became very involved with IGNITE and could be found at the camp serving others year after year.

Today, as Ish is beginning his new college life, his best friend Mario is in his second year of college at East Community College with a 3.8 GPA in engineering. Oh yeah, he's also 6'6" with the speed of a gazelle and quarterback on the football team. THAT'S RIGHT!

They are both special young men and anyone that comes around them can feel it as they constantly use their lives to serve others and live out daily what they know they've been called to do. Because of this, many lives have been changed. Including mine.

I am VERY proud of them.

A couple of summers after Ish and Mario first arrived at IGNITE, I met Tyler Opdyke on the first day of our summer sports camp. The look on this young ninth grader's face told you he didn't want to be there and to leave him alone.

Tyler was a kid who'd faced some very difficult times and describes himself as *"the average teenager lost and without direction in a world leading me on a path of certain destruction. Mad at the world and everything in it, I didn't care for authority and believed I didn't need anyone's help."* That was obvious, and he left camp that year almost just like he came.

To my surprise, Tyler showed up for another IGNITE sports camp the following summer and it was there that his world got rocked! Tyler's hard shell was slowly broken as he realized he did need help and God's love for him was beyond measure and would NEVER leave him despite his past. Accepting that God had an amazing plan for his life brought a change in young Tyler that everyone could see and feel. That plan was something Tyler stayed focused on and began bringing life to it.

Today, the kid who thought he may not make it out of high school is a football player at Mississippi College where he's studying to be a teacher and coach. When asked why he chose that profession he replied, "I want to be the father that many of these kids, like me, didn't have. What IGNITE did for me, I want to do for others."

That's exactly what Tyler is doing! He can be found at almost every IGNITE camp serving as a counselor and coach and constantly investing in the lives of others. God is using him in mighty ways and using the pain of his past to help walk others into their future with confidence and assurance.

Over the years the Lord has used IGNITE to play a small part in changing hundreds of lives. I could fill this book up with stories of incredible life transformations. But the truth is, for Ish and Mario, it started with a young Pastor Luke and his faithful team's commitment to live their Why week after week.

It was the dedication of men serving others with their gift of sports that helped steer Tyler towards becoming the man he was created to be.

Ish, Mario, Tyler, and MANY others are being used to help change lives by their willingness to be who they were created to be and not let their fears keep them from it! With each step, they grow more and more.

A collection of men and women living their Whys together can propel others AND themselves towards their destiny, but it starts by stepping out of the boat to serve others because this is what leads to fulfillment.

How are you serving others?

Are you serving in some form at work?

We've seen studies released over the past few years showing how disengaged workers are in the US. In fact, a 2017 post from Jim Clifton, Gallup Chairman and CEO, says only 30% of full-time workers in the US are engaged at work.

People tell me all the time their job is not somewhere they can live their purpose, but when asked to describe how it's preventing them from doing so they can rarely state specific examples. Answers like "I just can't" or "I don't have time" usually follow and occasionally the "My boss won't let me" sneaks in.

LIVING out your purpose ONLY requires that you do one thing. Get started! That's it! Yet for so many, this seems impossible to know how or where to begin and this lack of information and approach are usually the barriers keeping you from that first step to living out your purpose.

Do you know the Why of the company you work for? Can you state it clearly?

Do you know the Why of your employees?

The overwhelming answer to this question is NO and that's why so few people are engaged at work.

These questions are vitally important to the level of fulfillment by you or the employees of your organization. Remember, **people have an innate need to pursue fulfillment over happiness and WILL eventually go where fulfillment is found.** That's why so many companies have such high turnover rates and why so many individuals jump from one job to another and usually with no knowledge of why they're leaving. When asked, they all too often give answers like "I just didn't feel happy" or "It just got stale." We've all heard "I just needed something new."

So often a simple shift in our approach changes how we see things and can turn a dull job into one you love and are deeply fulfilled by. Let's try something. For the next week, I want to ask you to try this approach for me.

First, take the list of your top five core values from Chapter 3 and make them visible at work, on your desk, computer screen, in your vehicle, etc. Now with every task or job duty throughout the day find a way to connect them with one of your core values and WRITE THEM DOWN. Here's what I mean.

Let's assume you're a sales rep and not really excited about your job. Your core values are: change, teamwork, personal growth, service, and family.

The mandatory 5 p.m. daily conference call with your manager and region makes you nuts and only adds to your loss of excitement. Rather than dreading it and waiting for the call to end, listen intently to your teammates and find ways to add value to them (teamwork). Maybe even go home and research a potential solution to a problem they're having and present it on tomorrow's call (service). You could also share a motivational quote with the team before the call ends (growth).

This is just one example, but you get the point.

Another change of **APPROACH** is called **job crafting** and it's the practice of helping employees make subtle changes to how they do their scope of work. These changes often shift the mindset to focus more on meaning and purpose. Most people assume their job responsibilities are fixed but those responsibilities are usually more adjustable than they realized. Many employers recognize this and provide the opportunity for job crafting. No employer wants the headache of losing a good employee.

Watch for the trap of thinking your purpose is ALWAYS specific to your JOB. **Your purpose is specific to YOU and should permeate EVERY area of your life because it's the motivation behind everything you do.**

Think about what we said earlier in the book. God has put those passions, desires, strengths, and gifts in you, so you can serve His people. That's why it brings fulfillment.

For years we've watched counselors come to serve at IGNITE camps and it's as if a light switch turns on in them. They come alive because that's what happens to a life lived on purpose.

BEN'S STORY OF TRANSFORMATION

One of the most powerful transformations I've ever seen is my friend Ben Craddock. Ben played football at Ole Miss and now has a very successful business with his brother David. He has a gift of connecting with people and a passion for sports.

His pathway to purpose began by serving in the church nursery with his wife, Hillary. If you know Ben, then you'll understand how funny this is because he's completely ripped and looks like he's still playing college football. Those kids must have thought he was the Hulk!

Anyway, this eventually led to him serving at one of the

IGNITE summer sports camps where, in his words, the "light-bulb of significance" went off and he discovered his purpose.

Ben's Why is for people to know that God loves them and nothing in their past or future can change that. This is his motivation and is seen in every aspect of his life and the life of his company Craddock Oil. Because of this, lives all over Mississippi are being changed. Sports camps, fundraisers, blood drives, sponsorships, and community events are just a few things being fueled by this Why.

Recently I asked Ben what it's like to know his Why and he quickly responded, "Man it's who I am, and I'm so blessed to get to wake up each day and live it."

Ben had no idea his Why would ever have such an impact on his community and state. As I type this, an article just came out about him in the local paper and he's on his way to speak at a local high school.

Did Ben make out some strategy to get to this point? No. Did he have some big plan drawn out to get the recognition? Of course not. The truth is he could care less about all that. What he cares about is being true to the person he's been called to be with the resources God has given him.

Remember, his Why started in the church nursery scaring the little kids. Okay, well maybe not! But it did start with a simple plan to serve others.

When you discover and become who God created you to be and take the steps He asks you to then you will fulfill the journey you are meant to travel on through life.

"I believe purpose is something for which one is responsible; it's not just divinely assigned."

—MICHAEL J. FOX, *ALWAYS LOOKING UP: THE ADVENTURES OF AN INCURABLE OPTIMIST*

FOCUS AND IMPLEMENTATION REMINDERS:

Your purpose is specific to YOU and should permeate EVERY area of your life because it's the motivation behind everything you do.

A collection of men and women living their Whys together can propel others AND themselves towards their destiny, but it starts by stepping out of the boat to serve others.

People have an innate need to pursue fulfillment over happiness and WILL eventually go where fulfillment is found.

NEW APPROACH:

1. Before getting out of bed each morning, say this to yourself five times: "I am purpose driven!"

2. Find one way to implement your Why into EVERYTHING you do. This will take some time so DON'T get frustrated. Be creative and just GET STARTED!

Chapter 8
DISTRACTIONS AND
TEMPTATIONS

"Excellence is an art won by training and habituation. We do not act rightly because we have virtue or excellence, but rather have those because we have acted rightly. We are what we repeatedly do. Excellence, then, is not an act but a habit."

—ARISTOTLE

I feel like I know Mr. Distractions well considering he shows up every time I turn around. Over the years he's disguised himself in several different ways like surgeries, procedures, pain, medical bills, worries, people, etc.

Several years ago, the surgeries and procedures, aka distractions, seemed to be coming at speeds faster than we could keep up and you could see it on the faces of everyone in the family. Polly was on a roller coaster of nursing me back to health while taking care of our three small children, working a full-time job, and somehow cooking dinner when she got home. I know and you're right ... She's Wonder Woman (her company even gave her a Wonder Woman plaque!). I still don't know how she did it.

I could tell everyone needed a break and a change of scenery ASAP, but I was scheduled for another surgery the next week. To say we were distracted was an understatement. At that point, our lives were one big distraction, so we decided to get distracted from the distractions.

Following my surgery and hospital stay, we did exactly what you'd think. BEACH TRIP!!

My in-laws Ray and Susan loaded up our kids, Polly took an air mattress and made me a sweet bed in the back of the Suburban, and off we rolled! I know that sounds crazy and it was, but I decided I could heal up anywhere. Plus, Susan's a nurse so I was good.

Sometimes the only way to fight distractions is planning a distraction because planned distractions often provide the clarity for developing a new approach.

Distractions to your purpose come in all shapes and sizes and experience tells me the two most common distractions are OURSELVES and OTHERS.

"How am I the problem?" is usually the first thing out of someone's mouth when they hear they may be the distraction. The answers to that question are endless but here are just a few....

Some people are held hostage by their past and can't—no, WON'T—move forward into the life God has planned for them. God did NOT create you to dwell in the past and allow it to keep you from the future He has planned for you. He tells us that in 2 Cor. 5:17: *Therefore if anyone is in Christ, he is a NEW creation. The old is GONE and the new has COME.*

Your past is not meant to dictate your future and you can't truly move forward until you've dealt with it.

What does that look like for you? Is there someone in your life you need to forgive? Is it a friend, family member, co-worker? Is it you?

Whoever or whatever it is, it's time to deal with it and move forward into your destiny. Unforgiveness is like a weight resting on your shoulders and it will continue to slow you down and hold you captive until YOU decide to defeat it by releasing it through forgiveness and moving forward into the life created for you.

What about your schedule? Is it a distraction? Is it running your life? Most people say yes but the truth is they won't be still and they keep ALLOWING their schedules to run their lives instead of them running their schedules.

It's very easy to slip into this mode of operation and I've found myself there many times. The solution is to make a decision and have the guts to get it done!

Okay, I know I'm wearing out that saying but it's true and it's what I use to guide my life when I get off track or have to make a hard decision.

Guess what?? IT WORKS!!

Take control of your schedule and put a value on your time because your time is valuable, so don't let others rob you of it!

Another way we distract ourselves is our FEAR of failure. I once heard the acronym of FEAR is False Emotions Appearing Real. I love that because that's exactly what it is. We're even told in the Bible (2 Tim 1:7) that God didn't give us a spirit of fear, but He gave us a spirit of power, love, and a sound mind!

It's time to ditch the fear and live in that power! We MUST STOP ALLOWING our fear of failure to keep us from moving forward. I say over and over that without my failures I wouldn't know anything. There's no better way to learn to embrace it and get moving!

Do you allow OTHERS to keep you from your Why? Most people do. "What do you mean Chris?" you ask.

We often allow others to keep us from our Why because we're too worried about what they think or scared they won't approve of us. I get it and I've even been there. As we said earlier in the book, a transformation is scary because we don't yet know that person and when that happens it can feel like we're living in a glass house being watched all the time.

But the truth is **there will ALWAYS be people that are resistant to you living YOUR purpose.** Their resistance is ultimately fueled by THEIR fears.

THEIR fears are THEIR problem. NOT YOURS!

As we say at IGNITE, **"Average people want you to stay average and we will NOT let their fear of failure keep us from our destiny!"**

My friend Billy Alsbrooks said it best at our recent IGNITE Team 10 camp, *"Every second that you're worried about the opinions of others is a second you're losing. Stay focused and build your vision!"*

Don't let someone else's fears keep you from being who YOU were CREATED TO BE!

Whatever the distraction is, it comes down to your plan... your APPROACH. What is it? Do you have a plan? Do you have an approach? You've been given the gift of life and you've got ONE shot. Put together the APPROACH and begin executing!

TERRY'S APPROACH

With day one of camp in full swing, the pool was full of kids laughing when I noticed Terry sitting in the corner by himself and obviously mad about something. Terry came to us from a boy's home we'd given scholarships to. Fighting, stealing, getting kicked out of school, and arrested is what got him to the boy's home. I walked over and asked if he wanted to get in the pool and he quickly responded, "My momma told me don't trust nobody!" I tried talking to him, but he just stared at the ground and ignored me. The next several days followed the same path of little to no meaningful conversation.

Ted DiBiase Jr. was speaking one night, and I watched as Terry's eyes followed every word. Ted shared what it took for him to become a WWE superstar. The ups and downs and struggles to overcome along the way. Finding out that Ted walked out to 74,000 people at WrestleMania and was the star of the movie *The Marine 2* caused the campers to go nuts! High fives went up everywhere followed by cheers of excitement! They were fired up.

Ted quickly fueled the crowd. "The limos, jets, TV, movies, and money," he said as the crowd escalated further into a frenzy, "it means NOTHING to me compared to my relationship with Christ and I'd give it all up right now if He told me to!" And like THAT the room fell silent. All eyes were glued to the WWE star.

After a long pause, Ted went on to share about his biggest failures and screw-ups, as he called them, and then explained God's grace in a way that many, including Terry, quickly took hold of. Lives all over the room changed that night and Terry proudly gave his life to the Lord. A few days later, as camp came to an end, Terry, with excitement in his voice and life in his eyes, came to tell me all about it.

I didn't hear from Terry for two years. And then I got a letter from him telling me he was graduating high school and that he had missed camp because he'd gotten a job working at the grocery store for the last two years. I could feel his excitement through his words! He asked if we would come up to his graduation and proudly spoke of having the highest grades in the class in algebra and biology. *Was this the same Terry from camp?* I thought as I smiled.

Soon after I got a letter from one of his teachers bragging on his tremendous work ethic and about the amazing change that happened in him. "A change that may have even saved his life!" she said. A phone call with her revealed Terry had been going to church and even sang in the choir! He helped others in need and, in her words, he was the model student and a respectful young man. I must have read that letter 100 times! I was blown away.

As Dobby, Todd, and I made the drive through the Mississippi Delta, we could hardly contain our excitement as we planned to surprise Terry. I wish you could've seen the smile on Terry's face when he turned the corner, proudly wearing his cap and gown, and saw us standing there! He hugged each one of us and then introduced us to his friends. As one friend walked off he pointed at Todd, made a throwing motion with his arm and mouthed "pitched in the pros!" The excitement was in the air.

As Terry's name was called, he stood tall and proudly walked across that stage to get his diploma! Todd, Dobby, and I just looked at each other. No words needed to be exchanged and in silence, we each took in the magnitude of what we were seeing. It almost didn't seem real because the young man we were seeing was not the same man we met a couple of years earlier. He was being transformed into the person he was created to be.

It's something I'll NEVER forget.

Terry, if you're reading this I'm so proud of you for having the courage to become that person! Thank you for your inspiration.

You see when Terry left IGNITE to go back to the boy's home, his life HAD changed but the world he was going back to had not. Because of that, he needed a new approach to how he was going to live his new Why so that he could overcome the temptations and distractions he knew he would face. Was it easy? NO. Did he do it? YES.

How? His APPROACH!

Your approach is your weapon in the war on distractions!

What's your approach?

"Deep within each one of us there is an inner longing to live a life of *greatness* and contribution—to really matter, to really make a difference. We may doubt ourselves and our ability to do so, but I want you to know of my deep conviction that *you can* live such a life. You have the potential within you. We all do. It is the birthright of the human family."

—STEPHEN COVEY, *THE 8TH HABIT: FROM EFFECTIVENESS TO GREATNESS*

FOCUS AND IMPLEMENTATION REMINDERS:

Sometimes the only way to fight distractions is planning a distraction because planned distractions often provide the clarity for developing a new approach.

Your past is not meant to dictate your future and you can't truly move forward until you've dealt with it.

Unforgiveness is like a weight resting on your shoulders and it will continue to slow you down and hold you captive until YOU decide to defeat it by releasing it through forgiveness and moving forward into the life created for you.

There will ALWAYS be people that are resistant to you living YOUR purpose.

Don't let someone else's fears keep you from being who YOU were CREATED TO BE!

Your APPROACH is your weapon in the war on distractions!

NEW APPROACH:

1. Fine tune your weapon daily by taking time to reflect on what worked and what didn't.

2. Begin to filter out anyone in your life that hinders you from your purpose and surround yourself with those that push you towards it!

Chapter 9
PERSONAL MANIFESTO

"Where there is no vision, the people perish: but he that keepeth the law, happy is he."

—PROVERBS 29:18, *KING JAMES VERSION (KJV)*

Bo Trebotich, aka DJ Cadillac, has a life story unlike anything I've ever heard. A high school athlete with plans of playing in college, then one night a single bad decision landed him in jail and crushed his dream.

When he got out of jail he started playing music, got signed to a major record label, and toured the country with national acts playing to crowds of thousands of people.

After living the rock star life, he found himself involved in a bad business deal that left him completely broken and soon searching for his Why. Depression hit and amplified the struggle even more. One night, feeling his life had no value or meaning and seeing no way out, he began thinking of doing the unthinkable and made plans to end his suffering.

"Man, I was in bad, bad, place and just before it got real,"

Cadillac shared, "my best friend Jason Anderson, aka DJ Uri, walked in on me. One of the first things he said was he couldn't and would NOT live this life without me. Why would he say that? Was he really not willing to live his life if I wasn't around? He couldn't live without me?

"Man, Jason was my saving grace cause he's a husband and a dad and it showed me right then that I had people that truly care about me. It showed me my life was about way more than money and fame. He saved my life by showing how much he cared," Cadillac says with a big smile.

Soon after, Cadillac found his way to an IGNITE sports camp and spent four days serving the campers and sharing his struggles. Campers were blown away by his story and his commitment to them. A deep connection was felt and began to stir something inside Cadillac that brought a deeply felt joy.

Leaving camp was not the end to serving others for Cadillac. In fact, it was just the beginning. That connection led to him serving people in any fashion he could. It led to him discovering his Why.

Today he'll tell you he lives his life to bring glory to the Lord with a message of "What you go through today doesn't determine who you'll be tomorrow." Cadillac uses his personal story, gifts of sports, music, and passion for the outdoors to live out his Why. Because of this, thousands of teenagers have been exposed to this message and countless lives have been changed and saved! It's amazing to see!

Most people I know dream of making an impact like that. Do you? It's actually why you've been put on this Earth, but many never get to live it out because they get sidetracked, lose focus, or don't know where to start. That's WHY you need a Personal Manifesto.

So what is a Personal Manifesto?

A Personal Manifesto is a declaration of intentional living that states the intent of how you are going to live out your purpose or Why in your personal life. It naturally encourages you to follow through and is like having a vision board with you at all times.

Writing out your own Personal Manifesto will get you excited and keep you on track to living the life you were meant to live and being the person you were created to be!

Five things to have in your Personal Manifesto:

1. State your Why
2. List your core values
3. Declare your Belief Statement
4. State your intent or approach
5. Daily declarations

These five things and whatever else you want to add, should become the filter for EVERYTHING you do and every decision you make.

My Personal Manifesto looks like this:

WHY: Help people discover and become who God created them to be.

VALUES: Faith, family, courage, love, integrity, and fun.

APPROACH: The AAA Strategy: **Awareness, Approach, Attack.** Visit kellumbrothers.com for more on this.

DAILY DECLARATIONS:

1. Start today with Jesus
2. Stand and be who God created you to be
3. Expect more from yourself than others do
4. Love when others can't
5. Live IN integrity
6. Have fun

BELIEF STATEMENT: Greatness lies within each person and is found on the road of truth that everyone deserves to travel.

This Personal Manifesto provides the guardrails for which I live my life within. I say the daily declarations to myself consistently and ask God for the strength to live within these guardrails. This is the filter for all my decisions and that's why they're called my guardrails.

Now let's reflect on **you,** and **clarify and verify** your Personal Manifesto:

YOUR PERSONAL MANIFESTO

Your WHY:

_____

_____

_____

_____

_____

_____

Your VALUES:

_____

_____

_____

Your APPROACH:

_____

_____

_____

DAILY DECLARATIONS:

1. _____

_____

2. _____

_____

3. _____

_____

4. _____

_____

5. _____

_____

BELIEF STATEMENT:

_____

_____

_____

THREE POTENTIAL SERVICE OPPORTUNITIES:

1. _____
_____
2. _____
_____
3. _____
_____

Describe in detail WHY you feel these opportunities will connect with you.

_____
_____
_____
_____
_____

Describe in detail HOW you will connect with these opportunities. List the steps you will take.

_____
_____
_____
_____
_____
_____
_____
_____

"Do you wait for things to happen, or do you make them happen yourself? I believe in writing your own story."

—CHARLOTTE ERIKSSON

FOCUS AND IMPLEMENTATION REMINDERS:

A Personal Manifesto is a declaration of intentional living that states the approach or how you are going to live out your purpose or Why in your personal life.

Your Personal Manifesto provides the guardrails to live your life within.

Your Personal Manifesto is always like having a vision board with you so you can stay focused on what matters.

NEW APPROACH:

Take pride in your belief statement. Speak it to yourself daily and share it with at least one person each day.

Chapter 10
PROFESSIONAL MANIFESTO

"Write the vision. Make it clear on tablets, so anyone can read it quickly."

—HABAKKUK 2:2

Bill Blair, my guitar jamming, rock climbing, red-headed, completely wide-open friend, has an avid love for the Lord and the outdoors. He also owns a company called Rocks to Rivers (rockstorivers.com) that helps leaders come alive with a saying of "Let's Go!" that focuses on "Let's" as in, you are not alone. Bill has spent years helping people come alive and reach levels they would have only dreamed possible. I've watched him do it in his own life and the lives of others for a long time.

In the early days of Rocks to Rivers, he was given the opportunity to sign a contract with an organization that would have made R2R a significant amount of money, but the problem was he was being asked to step outside their Why. I was with Bill when this happened and after about five seconds, he respectfully declined the business. When I asked him why he passed it up he simply responded, "Easy man, I can't do it and stay true to the vision I know God has called me to."

Bill is keenly AWARE who God has called him to be and of the APPROACH. With that clarity, he's able to **ATTACK** his mission head-on while limiting distractions. Yes, that contract would have been financially beneficial to his company but in the end, it would've been a distraction by taking time away from what he's been called to do.

Bill is helping individuals, couples, teams, and organizations come alive day after day by staying true to his purpose and the life God has called him to live. His Why permeates everything he does.

You see, your Why must do two things. First, it should permeate everything YOU do and every aspect of your life. Secondly, it should act as a filter for every decision you make. If it doesn't do these two things, then it's probably not your Why.

Implementing your Why into your profession is what I call a Professional Manifesto and this APPROACH is one of the keys to alignment within the organization. In addition to your Why, you must also state your values. **Purpose-led people and organizations know AND live their values.**

To live the life you were created to live starts with the values within you. **Organizations typically take on the personality of its leader, so the leader MUST know his/her values and their Why and they MUST bleed into that organization.** Where this does NOT happen is where you usually find the tension in the leader, management, employees, or all three. It may also be why you're unhappy or disengaged at work.

When your values and Why don't line up with the values and Why of your company then tension eventually follows.

That's why it's so important to have your own Professional Manifesto. Just like your Personal Manifesto, this is a document declaring your values and your Why and how you will incorporate those in your profession. Whether you're the owner, CEO, cleaning crew, or intern, you need a Professional Manifesto and it MUST be the filter of every decision you make professionally. Your decisions should NEVER be dictated by anything or anyone else and by filtering them through your Professional Manifesto you never compromise who you are!

For example, my values are faith, family, courage, love, integrity, and fun. My purpose, as I've stated previously, is to help people discover and become who God created them to be. In my Professional Manifesto, my values are the same as my Why, reading like this: ***Creating Cultures of Purpose and Alignment.*** I'm doing the same thing, but it's worded differently FOR alignment.

My Professional Manifesto includes a belief statement and daily declarations professionally. It also states goals and benchmarks I'm looking to achieve as well as identified areas of improvement. It's a living document that provides guidance professionally.

What is your Professional Manifesto? Do you have one? Failure to do so leads to a lack of clarity and that lack of clarity can keep you from experiencing fulfillment.

It doesn't matter how much you like your job or how well your business is doing, if it's failing to provide fulfillment then you WILL eventually do one of the following: Stop performing at your ideal level, get restless, and leave OR you'll stay until you retire and THEN look back and ask yourself why you stayed and wasted all that time.

Life is too short to live like that and it's ONLY up to you to live your Why in your profession. That begins with your Professional Manifesto.

Are you living out your purpose at work?

How would you operate in your job if you knew your company's purpose and values lined up with yours? How would your business operate if you knew your employee's purpose and values lined up with those of your company? That's easy. You would operate TOGETHER on a mission, meeting your finest hour day after day.

That's the goal of the Professional Manifesto. It provides AWARENESS and the APPROACH for you to live your Why professionally.

Let's look at a couple of examples of what living out your purpose looks like in business.

A good friend of mine, Byron Knight, owns a coffee shop called Sneaky Beans in Fondren, a community known as the arts district in Jackson, Mississippi. I once asked him to tell me about getting started and with pride he described the demands and sacrifices it took to get up and running. "Why Sneaky Beans?" I asked. He quickly responded, "Man, the Bean is all about making people happy. We just want to help people have a good day."

I was asking why the name Sneaky Beans, but he was answering Sneaky Beans' Why. That answer made a huge impression on me and I instantly knew it would be way more than a successful coffee shop. It is.

Anyone that's ever been in The Bean will describe it as a happy place, a "solid vibe" as one dude put it. It's a place that literally helps you have a good day and because of that awareness and clarity to their purpose and Why, Sneaky Beans is a staple business in the community and is not just a solid cup of coffee. It's an experience.

REI is a national retail outdoor cooperative that proudly declares themselves to be "purpose-driven" and states "We grow our business by furthering our purpose."

Consequently, they have made *Fortune* magazine's Top 100 Places To Work every year since the list began in 1998. When asked what it's like to work at REI, "it's a lifestyle" is the answer you'll hear from the employees.

Whether you're an average Joe like me, a community coffee shop, or a multi-million-dollar business, a keen awareness of your purpose and Why is what you need to propel you into being that person or company you've always dreamed of becoming.

That starts with your Professional Manifesto!

At Kellum Brothers, we help companies clarify and verify their purpose and ensure that there is alignment within the culture of your company so that you can fulfill your purpose.

For more detailed information visit kellumbrothers.com.

"Don't let making a living keep you from making a life."

—JOHN WOODEN

FOCUS AND IMPLEMENTATION REMINDERS:

A Professional Manifesto is a document declaring your values and Why and how you will incorporate those in your profession.

Implementing your Why into your profession is what I call a Professional Manifesto and this APPROACH is one of the keys to alignment within the organization.

When your values and Why don't line up with the values and Why of the company you work for or own, tension eventually follows.

Purpose-led people AND organizations know their values and Why.

NEW APPROACH:

1. Refuse mediocrity in your profession and acknowledge daily where and how you raised your standards.

2. Document the influence you see it having on others and review that document as often as needed for motivation and confirmation!

Chapter 11
THE SCIENCE OF PURPOSE

"As to science, we may well define it for our purpose as 'methodical thinking directed toward finding regulative connections between our sensual experiences.'"

—ALBERT EINSTEIN

On July 16, 2018, NBC news reported results from a study by Pew Internet & American Life Project showing approximately 80% of American Internet users, or about 93 million Americans, have searched for a health-related topic online and that number has increased 62% since 2001.

How do you feel about your health? Are you doing anything about it? I hope so.

Did you know there is also research showing a purpose-led life leads to better health? In fact, Dr. Dhruv Khullar at New York Presbyterian Hospital said, "Having purpose is linked to a number of positive health outcomes, including better sleep, fewer strokes and heart attacks, and a lower risk of dementia, disability, and premature death."

From possible decreased risks of getting Alzheimer's disease to improved coping skills and choice making, research is everywhere showing the health benefits from living a purpose-led life. One study by Patrick Hill and Nicolas Turiano called "Purpose In Life as a Predictor of Mortality Across Adulthood" talked about the possibilities of a decreased mortality rate! That's amazing!

You've heard me say that discovering your purpose begins with serving others. So often when I tell people that, I can immediatcly tell they aren't happy about what I'm saying. I've even heard someone say they don't *think* they'd like it. Is that you?

How do you feel about serving others?

What if I could prove to you that serving others could really make you happy? Would you try it??

Check this out...

I'm fascinated with the brain and all its complexities. I especially love the term Happiness Trifecta! Have you ever heard that term before? It just sounds cool to me!

The Happiness Trifecta, as described by Dr. Eva Ritvo in *Psychology Today*, consists of dopamine, serotonin, and oxytocin. In her description, "Serotonin is connected to sleep, digestion, memory, learning, and appetite. Dopamine is connected to motivation and arousal. Oxytocin, 'the cuddle hormone,' is among the most ancient of our neurochemicals and has a powerful effect on the brain and the body."

When you serve others, even something as simple as opening the door for someone, according to research, your brain releases the Happiness Trifecta. Now I don't know about you, but I want some of that! Who wouldn't??

Seriously, if you know that then why would you not serve others? Why would you not step out of your comfort zone?

The bottom line is this...

If you're looking for deep happiness, and I hope we all are, then start serving others! As my grandmother used to say...

There's proof in the pudding!

"For me, I am driven by two main philosophies: know more today about the world than I knew yesterday and lessen the suffering of others. You'd be surprised how far that gets you."

—NEIL DEGRASSE TYSON

Chapter 12
THE TREE OF LIFE

"If you're not making someone else's life better, then you're wasting your time. Your life will become better by making other lives better."

—WILL SMITH

Our neighborhood was filled with friends that loved spending time together. Our kids bounced from one house to the next usually looking for the best food or the best pantry to raid.

The "Tree of Life" was a simple seating area under some dimly lit oak trees in our neighbor's driveway. With the flip of a switch the tree would shine bright and like an SOS call, people everywhere knew to grab a glass of wine and head that way with the cries of laughter soon to follow.

Over the years the Tree of Life became a sacred place of safety, treasured conversations, healing, and therapy for many as we helped each other walk through life together. It also led to some seriously fun times!

There were numerous times over the years when I heard the laughter coming from the Tree of Life, yet my back pain was tempting me to isolate myself inside. **Pain often leads to the temptation for isolation.**

At some point over the years, everyone in the neighborhood seemed to be confronted with their own form of individual pain in one way or another. These times were often walked through under the Tree of Life as the friendships seemed to carry each other's burdens and make that walk easier to travel.

The Tree of Life taught us all many important life lessons over the years and if asked to describe those lessons, I suspect each person's description would look different. For me it's easy. **Cherish friendships, value the simple, and love your neighbor.**

Our neighborhood looks different now as kids have grown up and families moved away. It's now filled with new families. A new set of voices and cries of laughter dance through the air as kids race up and down the street on bicycles and scooters. Young moms and dads often not far behind pushing a baby stroller and desperately trying to keep up or find the last bit of energy needed to get through the day.

It's a time I remember all too well. A beautiful time where exhaustion and fulfillment go hand in hand. A time of new experiences and a time when fears of the unknown can quickly creep in. A time, more than anything, where friendships are needed but free time is scarce.

It's during this time of life when a sense of community is painfully needed and often desperately sought after.

God created us to be in a relationship with others. In fact, when Jesus was asked by the religious leaders what the greatest commandment was, He said: *"Love the Lord your God with all your heart, soul, and mind."* He then said, *"the second is like it: Love your neighbor as yourself."*

Loving and serving others brings fulfillment!

Are you loving your neighbor? How are you going to create a culture in your neighborhood or community that inspires people to live lives of fulfillment and to love others as themselves?

Think about this question for a minute...

Do you have a feeling of longing for something deep within you but don't know exactly what it is? Does that feeling keep reminding you it's there and it's not going away?

That feeling is there because you were meant to be part of something bigger than yourself. Are you? Do you want to get started but not sure what you can do? I suggest loving your neighbor by setting up a Tree of Life in your neighborhood and **invite them to join you. A simple invitation might be the first step to changing lives.**

The fruits of the Tree of Life are **friendships, love, compassion, truth, hope, faith, safety, and certainty.** When you love your neighbor with those fruits then fulfillment will follow and seeds will be planted for future growth.

Those leaders that love and serve others bleed passion. That passion is contagious and produces an energy that others feel and ultimately desire.

Have you ever been around someone who puts off this kind of energy? The next time you are, pay attention to what they do and the words they use. More than likely, they are focused on you and asking questions about your life, family, interest, etc. They are sowing seeds from the fruits of the Tree of Life.

Consistently serving others by simply focusing on them and showing you care produces an energy that can transform cultures of all sizes. These transformations start by a small shift of focus from ourselves to others. Try it and see what happens.

I sense the Tree of Life is once again getting ready to meet new faces, hear new stories, and wipe away the fear of the future, the anxiety of the present, and guilt from the past. Will it be in your neighborhood? Will you be the one who flips the switch to turn the light on?

What is the story of your life going to look like? It's up to you!

"Love is not patronizing, and charity isn't about pity, it is about love. Charity and love are the same—with charity you give love, so don't just give money but reach out your hand instead."

—MOTHER TERESA

FOCUS AND IMPLEMENTATION REMINDERS:

You were created to be in a relationship with others.

You were created to be part of something bigger than yourself.

Consistently serving others by simply focusing on them and showing you care, produces an energy that can transform cultures of all sizes.

Leaders that love and serve others bleed fulfillment.

You've been given gifts, talents, and resources that others need!

NEW APPROACH:

1. EACH DAY find a way to put someone else's needs above yours and serve them.

2. Find a way to be someone's miracle!

PART 3: Attack

Chapter 13
IGNITING A MOVEMENT

"A change is brought about because ordinary people do extraordinary things."

—BARACK OBAMA

That spring morning of 2008, we had no idea that meeting up for some coffee would lead to the birth of IGNITE.

One thing we've all realized since then is it wasn't what we did that fueled IGNITE, it was why we did it. The Why is what connected and what the Lord used to build this army.

The Bible says, *"Man makes his plans, but the Lord directs his steps"* and that's exactly what happened. God took a group of broken men whose Why was to use the gifts and passions He gave them to serve Him and from there, things exploded. It wasn't easy, and we've definitely seen some trials, but He's always provided.

I love the "Dancing Man" video. It's a video of a single man dancing by himself at a music festival. He's literally the only person dancing and he's JAMMING! Finally, someone joins in with him and for a while the two of them get their groove on.

Then someone else jumps in. Then another and another and suddenly hundreds of people race to join the dancing movement.

You can watch the video on YouTube at:

https://www.youtube.com/watch?v=fW8amMCVAJQ

That's what happens with purpose-led lives! They're contagious because they move people! That's what God has done with IGNITE! It's what He wants to do with you!

You have been put on this Earth for such a time as this and it's up to you to discover and become who God created you to be. THIS IS YOUR TIME!

Movements are ready to be started and lives are waiting to be changed by you! The Lord has incredible plans for you and all you have to do is connect to it. I know that someone is reading this right now and you're feeling something stirring inside you. That's your purpose waiting to come alive, to be let out of the cage to explode into your greatness.

The Lord took a simple sports ministry and used it to help change countless lives through Him!! The Bible says in Ephesians 3:20 that *God is able to do immeasurably more than we can ever ask or imagine with His power at work within us.*

That's exactly what happened.

You see, we were thinking it was all about the kids and it was and THEN God did immeasurably more. Men began to sacrifice vacation time and time with their families to come to serve others through IGNITE camps. The lives of counselors began to change, and bonds were formed with men seeking community and accountability.

One Saturday at camp a rainstorm kept us from going outside

for training, so we gathered in the conference room and had a Warrior Talk where we allowed anyone to stand up and share. One camper spoke of his plan to kill himself last year but his experience at camp changed his life and showed him how much God loved him. That love was so easily confirmed by the smile on his face. That one event changed the trajectory of that kid's life and saved him.

After hearing this, Carter, a counselor, stood up to share. Carter, whose wife Megan was diagnosed with terminal cancer, had a thriving business. To everyone's surprise, he shared his intent to walk away from that business to do what he felt God was telling him to do with the idea He'd given Carter. Carter said if the kids could be bold enough to step out for the Lord then so would he despite the fears of leaving a stable job while his wife fights cancer.

Today Habco, Carter's business, is thriving as he lives out his dreams.

I've often asked myself what would've happened if Carter had not served at that camp. In the midst of some serious struggles he chose to serve others and that "one decision," as Dave Jesiolowski says, changed not only his life, but the lives of many others as well.

The Lord is using WHY to fuel the IGNITE movement and propel it to places we never dreamed. Athletes, college students, business owners, ministers, first responders, servicemen, entertainers, musicians, and people from all walks are serving others together while helping each other navigate the roads of life. Lives are being RADICALLY changed, Whys found, relationships mended, lives saved, families restored, and it all started with a commitment to serving others.

I've heard it said many times that revolutions don't start because of what they do, they start from WHY they do it!

Are you ready to join a movement?

Step into your Why and JOIN the movement!!

My intent and the intent of Kellum Brothers is to IGNITE a movement of men, women, and organizations committed to intentionally IGNITING their purpose personally and professionally. Our goal is to create an army of 1,000,000 people in the next five years.

Will you be part of it?

Susan Scott says, "While no single conversation is guaranteed to transform a company, a relationship, or a life, any single conversation can."

Life or death decisions are being made every day. You just don't know that it's happening. Like the story about the boy that shared doing the Warrior Talk at IGNITE, you never know what might happen if you have a conversation with someone that ignites something in them that changes the trajectory of their life.

Are you willing to join the Igniting Your Purpose movement of men and women committed to living the lives they were created to live? Committed to living their Why?

Join the movement by registering at kellumbrothers.com and uploading a one-minute video of how you're living out your Why in your life personally and professionally.

One WINNER will be selected EACH month. To view what you can win by uploading your video, visit kellumbrothers.com.

We are committed to YOU and to IGNITING this movement. Why? Because, as I said earlier, YOU DESERVE IT! We believe in a God that does immeasurably more than we could EVER ask or imagine, and that begins with you!

During the reign of King David, there was a man named Eleazar who was one of the King's Mighty Men. Eleazar was a bad dude and once took on the Philistine army by himself and WON. Talk about defeating the odds!

Charles Spurgeon once said, *"DARE to stand alone! Dare to have a PURPOSE firm! Dare to MAKE IT KNOWN! Dare to be an Eleazar and GO FORTH and fight the Philistines alone; you will soon find that there are others in the house who have concealed their sentiments, but when they see YOU COMING forward, they will be openly on the Lord's side. Many cowards are skulking about trying to shame them. Many are undecided yet LET THEM SEE a brave man and he will be the STANDARD BEARER around whom they WILL rally."*

It's time to STAND with a courage like never before and be who you were created to be!!

Because you are meant to be the STANDARD BEARER!

"It had long since come to my attention that people of accomplishment rarely sat back and let things happen to them. They went out and happened to things."

—LEONARDO DA VINCI

FOCUS AND IMPLEMENTATION REMINDERS:

Purpose-led lives are contagious!

You have been put on this Earth for such a time as this and it's up to you to discover and become who God created you to be. THIS IS YOUR TIME!

Revolutions don't start because of WHAT you do, they start from WHY you do it!

Movements are ready to be started and lives are waiting to be changed by you!

NEW APPROACH:

Join the movement!

Chapter 14
LAUNCH AND ADJUST

"Your life does not get better by chance, it gets better by change."

—JIM ROHN

Thank you for taking this journey with me! We've made it to the final chapter. How are you feeling so far? Have you made any progress since starting? I certainly hope so!

I want to use this last chapter to tie up some loose ends and bring a little more clarity.

I love the phrase launch and adjust! It's a phrase my friend John Hugh Tate uses all the time and the truth is I stole it from him. John Hugh is the pastor of Bellwether Church and in the early days of Bellwether I must have heard him say this a thousand times and that's exactly what we did. Launch and adjust!

One of the things I love about John Hugh is his willingness to risk failure. He knows that nothing good comes from playing it safe and he's willing to take calculated risks. Sometimes those calculated risks pay off and sometimes they don't, which is where launch and adjust comes from. When the launch doesn't bring desired results, or you try something and you have no connection to it then you adjust.

The only way to know God's will for your life, your purpose, or your Why is to launch and adjust. In fact, it even says so in the Bible. *Romans 12:2 says "Do not conform to the pattern of this world but be transformed by the renewing of your mind. Then you can TEST AND APPROVE what God's will is for your life. His good pleasing and perfect will."*

What are you testing? Have you tested or launched into anything new lately? Have you tried something new only to realize you like one thing better than the other? That's the point and exactly what it's designed to do.

Until you launch and adjust, aka test and approve, you will NOT discover your purpose. Why? Because that's how God intended it to be. His will for your life is good, meaning it's good for you. It's pleasing, meaning you WILL LIKE IT, and it's perfect for you, meaning it's why you were created. Is there any part of that you don't want? I can't imagine there is.

Here's what I mean.

Music is a true passion of mine and I've played in bands most of my life. When Polly and I began serving in the church, she encouraged me to call the youth minister and tell him I played guitar in case he needed any help with the worship band. Reluctantly, I agreed, and it ended up totally changing my life. That's where I met that INSANE rocker dude and youth pastor (owner of Rocks to Rivers) named Bill Blair and he immediately plugged me in the band. By the way, he's INSANE in a good way.... I think!

Anyway, Bill and I hit it off and before long he challenged me to start leading worship. I did and it became a true passion of mine that I would've never known about had I not stepped out of my comfort zone, and trust me, that was a big step for me.

One night a young pastor named John Hugh Tate spoke to the youth group and a couple of years later he asked if Polly and I wanted to come with him and Linda to start a church where he would serve as pastor and I as worship leader. We agreed, built a team, and Bellwether Church was founded.

The point is this. Had I not been willing to launch and adjust, then my whole life would look different. Bill is now like a brother to me and serving with him in the youth ministry is how I met John Hugh, which led to the start of Bellwether Church. Bellwether was instrumental in helping us start IGNITE and both of them are what led me to my purpose in life. All that from a launch and adjust.

Where are you right now? Are you in need of launching into something? Do you need to test and approve? What's holding you back? You very well may be delaying the first step to your destiny. Your greatness could be right in front of you waiting for you to launch.

What if I launch and it's not what I was supposed to do? you're thinking.

You adjust and learn all you can from that experience by looking back at the notes you took along the way. Launch and adjust is the ONLY way you find clarity. It's the only thing that will bring you awareness to your current realities and that awareness is what you MUST have to walk into your purpose.

The only way I became so clear to my Why was by failing more times than I succeeded. FAILURE is NOT failure unless you don't learn anything from it. There is no greater resource in life than lessons learned from OUR failures because those lessons are not easily forgotten. These lessons are what bring awareness and awareness leads to discovery! Discovery is the fuel you need to propel you to your greatness and it starts with your willingness to launch out of your comfort zone and adjust with the discoveries made along the way.

What would the world look like right now if Henry Ford, the Wright brothers, Steve Jobs, Bill Gates, or Mark Zuckerberg had been scared to launch and adjust? How would society look if Rosa Parks had not refused to give up her seat on the bus that day in Montgomery, Alabama? What if fear kept Martin Luther King or Nelson Mandela from taking their first step?

You were meant to live to the fullest, the one life you've been created for, and your launch is what will get you there. The first step of your launch is to make the decision and have the guts to get it done! That's it and YOU CAN DO THIS! You've been waiting your whole life for this, so don't take it lightly. Remember, it starts by simply making a choice. Now MAKE THAT DECISION and get started! YOU DESERVE IT!

"There is no greater gift you can give or receive than to honor your calling. It's why you were born and how you become most truly alive."

—Oprah Winfrey

IGNITING YOUR PURPOSE
SEVEN-DAY CHALLENGE

Discovering your Why can be a challenge and takes some work. I want to ask you to take the next seven days and focus daily on the topic at hand. I've made daily challenge videos for you to watch at kellumbrothers.com. Each video has a corresponding question for you to answer in your journal. This exercise is meant to increase AWARENESS and get you mentally prepared to travel down the road to discovering your purpose.

START each day with this exercise then throughout the day document the connections by writing them in your journal.

At the end of the seven days, I want to ask you to shoot a quick thirty- to sixty-second video telling us about your connections and what you learned about yourself through this process. Email that video to chris@kellumbrothers.com for your chance to win three months of coaching sessions FREE valued at $2391.00 and a one-year subscription to our live monthly coaching membership program valued at $359.88. A total value of $2750.88.

Remember, YOU DESERVE THIS!!!

RECOMMENDED READING

Culture: *Fierce Conversations* by Susan Scott

Connecting: *One Question* by Ken Coleman

Leadership: *Extreme Ownership* by Jocko Willink

Business: *Tools of Titans* by Tim Ferris

Purpose: *Find Your Why* by Simon Sinek

Decision Making: *One Decision Can* by Dave Jesiolowski

Self-Image: *Psycho-Cybernetics* by Dr. Maxwell Maltz

All of the Above: The Bible

ACKNOWLEDGMENTS

John Maxwell said, "The dream is free, but the journey is not." I'm so thankful for this journey! Nothing about it has been easy and I would have never made it without these people as well as MANY others that aren't listed here.

First, I owe everything to the Lord. Thank you for providing the strength to make it and for sending many servants to lead me along the way.

Polly, you are my soulmate and there are no words to express the gratitude I have for what you've done for me. Thank you for your commitment and dedication to our family and your courage to live "in sickness and health" with grace, honor, and respect. You have sacrificed so much for me and given more than anyone will ever know. I love you!

To Riley, Reed, and Anna: my love for you is beyond measure and I praise God daily for giving you to me. You are my inspiration and I am so proud of who you have become! Never forget, your circumstances don't define who you are. You are a child of the Almighty God with His greatness inside you. LIVE IT!!

Mom and Dad thank you for demonstrating what a Godly marriage looks like and for displaying love in everything you do. You raised us in a house of love, respect, and hope. What you put up with ... WOW! I love you both so much!

To my brothers Kevin, Shane, and Clayton: you are my best friends and role models. Thank you! *SIDE NOTE: For clarity, you weren't my role models until sometime after each of your thirtieth through thirty-third birthdays. Before that ... NUTS!!*

Ray and Susan: thank you for allowing me to marry your daughter and for accepting me as a son. I am so blessed to have you in my life and to be part of your family. Thank you!

Dr. McGuire, you speak strength into me with every visit and your encouragement does more for me than you'll ever know. The day you put me on disability you told me I'd "see it" one day. I see it. Thank you!! You gave my life back and I will never be able to repay you.

To the IGNITE Board, Todd Dyess, Dobby Bowdon, Chris Snopek, Ben Craddock, Keith Lofton, and Jason Edwards: you guys are my heroes and I can't imagine doing this without you! Thank you for your commitment to serving the Lord! He continues to use you in MIGHTY ways and I am blessed to serve beside you.

Bellwether Church: thank you for your love and for being the body of Christ. You walked us through difficult times while never failing to show God's love! Thank you!

John Hugh and Linda Tate: thank you for your trust. Starting Bellwether and serving has been one of the greatest privileges of my life. It's an honor to serve with you. Thank you for your commitment to the Gospel and for your friendship.

Bill Blair: you are a brother to me and if it weren't for your encouragement I would have never started leading worship. God used you in more ways than you'll ever know. I am so blessed by your life. Thank you, brother!

ABOUT CHRIS

Chris lives in Jackson, MS with his wife Polly and their three kids, Riley, Reed, and Anna, and spent most of his career in the medical sales industry. In October 2008, after eight back surgeries, Chris' career was cut short as he was placed on long-term disability at just 38 years old due to degenerative disc disease, which ultimately led to ten spinal surgeries, dozens of procedures, a life dealing with pain, and what he calls "unusual circumstances."

Chris admits that being placed on disability was one of the hardest things he's ever been through but says he lives by the mantra "your circumstances don't define who you are." It was during this time that he helped start Bellwether Church, where he served as worship leader, and IGNITE Ministries, a sports and outdoors ministry for teenage boys. Through that journey, Chris found his life's calling of helping people discover and become who God created them to be.

Chris works with individuals and businesses through coaching, consulting, training, teaching, and speaking.

For additional information about Kellum Brothers products, services, or corporate job crafting call (769) 300-1294 or visit kellumbrothers.com.

To order more copies of this book for your company call (769) 300-1294 for bulk discount sales.

94104086R00069